Irish Independent
JANUARY 13, 1941.

DEATH OF JAMES JOYCE

JAMES JOYCE, the famous Irish-born writer, died in hospital in Zurich at 2.15 a.m. to-day. He was 58.

Though he was pronounced out of danger earlier yesterday, his condition became suddenly worse last night. Blood transfusions were given at once. On Saturday he had undergone an emergency abdominal operation.

MUCH DISCUSSED

James Joyce was one of the most discussed figures in contemporary literature.

Born on February 2, 1882, he was educated at Clongowes Wood and later at Belvedere College, and took his B.A. degree at the Royal University.

Even as a University student he became known as a writer, and he was regarded as one of the most brilliant students of his generation.

His chief publications before he went to live on the Continent were his collection of short stories "Dubliners" and his semi-autobiographical work, "The Portrait of the Artist as a Young Man."

NOTABLE BOOKS

Opinions about his later work vary, but there is general agreement that those two books were notable contributions to English literature and that they showed great imagination, a fine use of words, an extraordinary sensitiveness to the social, political, and religious life of the Dublin of that day.

When he left Ireland, not long before the 1914-18 war, he went first to Trieste, as a teacher, and later lived in Rome and Zurich before finally settling in Paris. His chief works of the Continental period were "Ulysses" and "Work in Progress," the latter published in fragments.

He had become hostile to the Catholic Church, in which he had been brought up. But in all his writings it seems as if he were never easy about his attitude to the Church, as if his quarrel with it preyed on his mind continually.

Visitors to him in Paris of late years have spoken of him as always being very much interested in news of Dublin and very fond of talking about his native city. They have described him as usually being dressed in white, and finding it necessary, owing to failing sight, to write with a great red pencil on huge sheets of paper.

His last book, "Work in Progress," was published about a year ago, though he had begun work on it as far back as 1923.

He married Nora, daughter of Thomas Barnacle, of Galway, in 1904. They had one son and one daughter.

THE IRISH TIMES
TUESDAY, JANUARY

JAMES JOYCE AS MAN AND ARTIST

TRIBUTES BY IRISH FRIENDS

By C. P. Curran

WITH Joyce dead in Zurich, and an end made to a forty years' friendship, one's thoughts inevitably revert to the first meeting. It was at my first lecture at University College. The class was in English literature, and the lecturer began with Aristotle's Poetics, as seemed to me very right in the circumstances. Towards the end of the lecture the professor put in some remark about Stephen Phillips, who had just written "Paolo and Francesca." He asked had anyone read it, and then immediately: "Have you read it, Mr. Joyce?" A voice behind me said "Yes"; I looked around, and saw my first poet.

I grew very familiar with that figure in the next three years, and in my eyes it did not change much in the next forty. Tall, slim and elegant; an erect and loose carriage, an up-tilted, long, narrow head, with a chin that jutted out arrogantly; firm, tight shut mouth, blue eyes that for all their myopic look could glare suddenly or stare with indignant wonder; a high forehead that bulged under stiff-standing hair. Some of these items changed later. The elegant adumbration of a beard tentatively came and went, and the eyes that since then saw and suffered so much were obscured by powerful lenses; but the graceful figure and carriage remained the same, and the cane that replaced the famous ash-plant of his later Dublin days still swung casually, disguising but aiding the dimmed vision.

That is how he looked in Paris, where he lived in the years between the two wars, in different apartments from the Faubourg to the Invalides. The talk within might be as much in Italian as in French, but there were pictures by Jack Yeats looking down from the walls—pictures, I need hardly say, of Anna Liffey—and above them a great wood-carving of the Arms of Dublin, that once looked out on the Liffey herself. And gradually the spirit of Dublin would prevail. He would sing old Tudor songs and Dublin street ballads in an admirable tenor voice, trained years before in Dublin by Signor Palmieri when he won distinction at the Feis Ceoil in 1904. I once asked Joyce when was he coming back to Dublin. "Why should I?" he said. "Have I ever left it?" And, of course, he never really had. He contained Dublin. His knowledge of the town by inheritance, by observation, by memory was prodigious, and he was at pains to keep his picture of it up to date.

WORTH HALF-A-DOZEN LEGATIONS

By Kenneth Reddin

The first time I met Joyce he was living in the Rue de Grenelle. I went down armed with a box of Olhausen's black puddings. I did this on Paddy Tuohy's advice—I mean on the advice of my friend, the late Patrick Tuohy, R.H.A., at that time living in Paris, having completed the now famous portrait of Joyce's father and one of Joyce himself. Tuohy wired me just in time. James's birthday was approaching. He loved Olhausen's black puddings. They recalled his student days in Dublin. So I came armed with them, and Tuohy and I enjoyed them, too, that night in the Rue de Grenelle.

I was the Irish delegate to the International Congress of P.E.N. in Paris in 1937. Immediately I arrived Joyce rang me. He subsequently attended one of the meetings, receiving an ovation, and delivered a speech on the pirated editions of "Ulysses" in America. At the banquet held at the close of the Congress he personally organised an Irish table, presided at it and, again receiving an ovation from a very distinguished literary gathering, made a short speech in reply to the toast 'Ireland.' Afterwards in the foyer in the hotel a whole world of writers surrounded him.

Joyce was worth half a dozen Irish Legations in any country he had chosen to live in. All European writers knew of him, and he took care to let them know that he was Irish. In making Dublin famous he made Ireland famous in European letters.

MEMOIR OF THE MAN

By Arthur Power

It was with a shock that I read of the death of James Joyce in the *Irish Times* this morning. Bad news travels quickly even in war-time, and, in spite of the numerous difficulties, people have been asking since the surrender of Paris what had happened to James Joyce and where he was. Now we hear from Zurich that he is dead.

It is hard to write of a man whom one knew well, and who was a true and great friend, while still under the blow of his loss. For Joyce was a gentle and affectionate man who loved his friends, and, in turn, was loved by them. A stray and unknown Irishman in Paris, I experienced, for no other reason but affection, a constant kindness from him, while living very much alone there, for a number of years—years during which he was at the peak of his international fame: a fame which, though he appreciated it, never swerved him to forget the simple and real things of life—his family and his personal friends. His natural nobility was too great to have his balance of life upset by his rise to fame, though a fame as remarkable and widespread as any Irishman has experienced abroad.

A SIMPLE MAN

For though in intellect he was complicated by nature, he was a simple man: and a man of fine and delicate sensibility, as an artist must be. Indeed, his genius consisted of two main characteristics—great originality and great sensibility, which amounted to almost super-sensitiveness in his case. As a result, he avoided all excess and lived a very simple life. The programme of his day, when I knew him twenty and fifteen years ago, was generally as follows: He rose fairly late, unless there was purpose otherwise, and generally he went out to lunch in a neighbouring restaurant. After lunch he would return to his flat, somewhere about three, and work until six or seven in the evening; then he used to collect his family and go to dine at the restaurant of a Monsieur Casabelle, close to the Gare Montparnasse. There he would dine sparingly: the chief interest of the dinner being in the wine, of which he was a connoisseur. He would remain there until about nine-thirty, when he would return to his flat, near the Champs de Mars, where he used to remain until twelve or one in the morning discussing literature and various artistic personalities we knew. That was his

Document 20:
Extracts from notices of the death of James Joyce, *Irish Independent*, 13 January 1941; *Irish Times*, 14 January 1941.

James Joyce died in Zurich early in the morning of 13 January 1941. The three main Dublin newspapers reported the event that day, and the following day the *Irish Times* had a feature with contributions from three Irishmen, all writers in their own right, who knew Joyce well.

The photograph below shows Joyce and Nora Barnacle with their solicitor on the day of their marriage in London, 4 July 1931. The *Irish Independent* notice states that they married in 1904 but their common law arrangement was not regularised until 1931.

The following extract from *A Portrait of the Artist as a Young Man* (Chap. V) may sum up Joyce's own view of his function in life —

— Look here, Cranly — he said.— You have asked me what I would do and what I would not do. I will tell you what I will do and what I will not do. I will not serve that in which I no longer believe, whether it call itself my home, my fatherland or my church: and I will try to express myself in some mode of life or art as freely as I can and as wholly as I can, using for my defence the only arms I allow myself to use, silence, exile and cunning.—

the proxenete! Proxente and what is that? Were you never at school? It's just the same as if I was ... to go for example now ... proxenete you. For God' sake! ous is that what she is?

O tell me all about Anna Livia ! I want to hear all about Anna Livia.
Well, you know Anna Livia ? Yes, of course, we all know Anna Livia. Tell
me all. Tell me now. You'll die when you hear. Well, you know, when
the old chap went ^phut and did what you know. Yes. I know, go on. Wash away
and don't be dabbling. Tuck up your sleeves and loosen your talktapes. Or
whatever it was they try to make out he tried to do in the Phoenix park.
He's an awful old rep. Look at the shirt of him ! Look at the dirt of it !
He has all my water black on me. And it steeping and stuping since this
time last week. How many times is it I wonder I washed it ? I know by
heart the places he likes to soil. Scorching my hand and starving my
famine to make his private linen public. Wallop it well with your battle
and clean it. My wrists are rusty rubbing the mouldy stains. And the
loads of wet and the sewers of sin in it ! what was it he did at all ? It
was put in the papers what he did. But time will tell. It know it will.
Time and tide will wash for no man. O, the old old rep ! What age is he at

M who told you that jackalantern's tale? My gabbard be carried.

^And how long was he under lough and neagh?
^It ^at all on Annual Sunday

O
tell me all about
Anna Livia! I want to hear all about Anna
Livia. Well, you know Anna Livia? Yes, of
course, we all know Anna Livia. Tell me
all. Tell me now. You'll die when you hear.
Well, you know, when the old cheb went
futt and did what you know. Yes, I know,
go on. Wash quit and don't be dabbling.
Tuck up your sleeves and loosen your talktapes. And don't, butt me—hike!—when
you bend. Or whatever it was they threed to

3

Document 19:
Extract from a page of the first typescript of *Anna Livia Plurabelle. (National Library Ms. 17,820)*

In 1923 Joyce began 'Work in Progress' of which extracts were published at various times in periodicals and in limited editions, partly to protect copyright. It was completed in 1938 and the entire work was published the following year with the title *Finnegans Wake*. The *Anna Livia Plurabelle* section was first published in book form in New York in 1928 in an edition which had a preface by Padraic Colum; the first page of that edition is reproduced so that the draft typescript can be compared with the final version. Joyce usually made several drafts of all his writings and put in lengthy additions first to the manuscripts, then to the typescripts and also in most cases to the printer's proofs; he calculated that he wrote up to one third of *Ulysses* in the form of additions to the printer's proofs.

The photograph below shows Joyce with three of his associates: the English novelist Ford Madox Ford who published parts of 'Work in Progress' in his periodical *transatlantic review* (Paris); the American poet Ezra Pound who promoted Joyce's literary reputation; John Quinn of New York, the famous Irish-American lawyer who defended the publishers of the *Little Review* in 1921 when they were prosecuted for publishing *Ulysses*. The photograph was taken at Pound's rooms in Paris in 1923.

UNITED STATES DISTRICT COURT

Southern District of New York

------------------------------x

    United States of America,

        Libelant

        v.   OPINION

    One Book called "Ulysses"   A. 110-59
    Random House, Inc.,

        Claimant

------------------------------x

    <u>On cross motions for a decree in a libel of confiscation, supplemented by a stipulation - hereinafter described - brought by the United States against the book "Ulysses" by James Joyce, under Section 305 of the Tariff Act of 1930, Title 19 United States Code, Section 1305, on the ground that the book is obscene within the meaning of that Section, and, hence, is not importable into the United States, but is subject to seizure, forfeiture and confiscation and destruction.</u>

United States Attorney - by Samuel C. Coleman, Esq. and Nicholas Atlas, Esq., of
    counsel - for the United States, in support of motion for a decree of forfeiture, and in opposition to motion for a decree dismissing the libel.

Messrs. Greenbaum, Wolff & Ernst, - by Morris L. Ernst, Esq., and Alexander Lindey,
    Esq., of counsel - attorneys for claimant Random House, Inc., in support of
    motion for a decree dismissing the libel, and in opposition to motion for a
    decree of forfeiture.

    I am quite aware that owing to some of its scenes "Ulysses" is a rather strong draught to ask some sensitive, though normal, persons to take. But my considered opinion, after long reflection, is that whilst in many places the effect of "Ulysses" on the reader undoubtedly is somewhat emetic, nowhere does it tend to be an aphrodisiac.

    "Ulysses" may, therefore, be admitted into the United States.

December 6, 1933

                                                        John M. Woolsey
                                                  United States District Judge

Document 18:
Opinion of Judge John M. Woolsey that *Ulysses* is importable into the United States, 6 December 1933. *(National Library Ms. 18, 539)*

Shakespeare and Company brought out a number of editions of *Ulysses* and by 1930 it had published over 28,000 copies. The book was vehemently attacked from many quarters and in Ireland while it was never officially banned most shops would not stock it. It was banned in the United States and indeed most of the several hundred copies of the first edition which reached American readers in 1922 were imported secretly and illegally, a number of them being smuggled in from Canada by an associate of Joyce's friend Ernest Hemingway. There was obviously a market for *Ulysses* in the United States and an unscrupulous publisher pirated it. First he serialised it in a periodical and later brought it out in book form and sold it illegally without paying royalties to Joyce. Eventually Joyce gave the contract for an American edition to the New York publisher, Random House. The authorities had banned the book on the grounds that it was obscene but when Random House tested the issue in court the judge found in favour of *Ulysses* and allowed it to be imported or published in the United States. The document recording his decision runs to eight pages of which the introduction and final paragraphs are reproduced.

The photograph below shows Sylvia Beach, the original publisher of *Ulysses,* discussing business with Joyce in Shakespeare and Company. The posters refer to two reviews of *Ulysses* published in April 1922. The *Sporting Times* (sub-titled *The Pink 'Un*) featured an attack on the book, while the literary periodical *Outlook* carried a balanced and generally favourable review by the English novelist and critic Arnold Bennett. The photograph is courtesy of the James Joyce Tower Museum, Sandycove, Dublin.

ULYSSES

by

JAMES JOYCE

SHAKESPEARE AND COMPANY
12, Rue de l'Odéon, 12
PARIS

1922

Stately, plump Buck Mulligan came from the stairhead, bearing a bowl of lather on which a mirror and a razor lay crossed. A yellow dressinggown, ungirdled, was sustained gently behind him by the mild morning air. He held the bowl aloft and intoned :

— *Introibo ad altare Dei.*

Halted, he peered down the dark winding stairs and called up coarsely :

— Come up, Kinch. Come up, you fearful Jesuit.

Solemnly he came forward and mounted the round gunrest. He faced about and blessed gravely thrice the tower, the surrounding country and the awaking mountains. Then, catching sight of Stephen Dedalus, he bent towards him and made rapid crosses in the air, gurgling in his throat and shaking his head. Stephen Dedalus, displeased and sleepy, leaned his arms on the top of the staircase and looked coldly at the shaking gurgling face that blessed him, equine in its length, and at the light untonsured hair, grained and hued like pale oak.

Buck Mulligan peeped an instant under the mirror and then covered the bowl smartly.

— Back to barracks, he said sternly.

He added in a preacher's tone :

— For this, O dearly beloved, is the genuine Christine : body and soul and blood and ouns. Slow music, please. Shut your eyes, gents. One moment. A little trouble about those white corpuscles. Silence, all.

He peered sideways up and gave a long low whistle of call then paused awhile in rapt attention, his even white teeth glistening here and there with gold points. Chrysostomos. Two strong shrill whistles answered through the calm.

— Thanks, old chap, he cried briskly. That will do nicely. Switch off the current, will you ?

Document 17:
Title page and first page of text of *Ulysses*, Paris, 1922.

The novel *Ulysses* celebrating the adventures of Leopold Bloom on 16 June 1904 was begun in 1914. While still incomplete it was serialised in the *Little Review* in New York in 1918-19, but some issues of the periodical were confiscated by the United States Post Office, and the Society for the Prevention of Vice succeeded in stopping its publication. In London Harriet Weaver published five instalments in the *Egoist* in 1919, and tried to have it published in book form but could find no printer willing to undertake such a risky project. However, in Paris a young American Sylvia Beach, proprietor of the bookshop Shakespeare and Company, succeeded in publishing an edition of 1000 copies on 2 February 1922, Joyce's birthday.

The photograph below (National Library, Lawrence Collection Cab. 2917) shows the Martello Tower, Sandycove, where the opening scene of *Ulysses* is set. Joyce lived in the Tower for some weeks in September 1904 as guest of Oliver St. John Gogarty (Buck Mulligan in *Ulysses*) who had it leased at the time.

16

Document 16:
Photographs of the Joyce family, 1905–24.

During this period the family lived mainly in Trieste and Zurich and in Paris to which they moved in 1920. The first photograph shows James' brother Stanislaus who went to live with him in Trieste in 1905. The second shows Nora with her children Giorgio and Lucia in Zurich about 1916. Below are James, Giorgio, Lucia and Nora, photographed in Paris about 1924.

The photographs are from the following sources: an original formerly in the possession of Stanislaus' wife Mrs. Nelly Joyce; University of Buffalo Library; University College Dublin Library, C.P. Curran Papers.

EXILES

A PLAY IN THREE ACTS

BY

JAMES JOYCE

LONDON
GRANT RICHARDS LTD.
ST MARTIN'S STREET
1918

EXILES

FIRST ACT

The drawingroom in Richard Rowan's house at Merrion, a suburb of Dublin. On the right, forward, a fireplace, before which stands a low screen. Over the mantelpiece a gilt-framed glass. Further back in the right wall, folding doors leading to the parlour and kitchen. In the wall at the back to the right a small door leading to a study. Left of this a sideboard. On the wall above the sideboard a framed crayon drawing of a young man. More to the left double doors with glass panels leading out to the garden. In the wall at the left a window looking out on the road. Forward in the same wall a door leading to the hall and the upper part of the house. Between the window and door a lady's davenport stands against the wall. Near it a wicker chair. In the centre of the room a round table. Chairs, upholstered in faded green plush, stand round the table. To the right, forward, a smaller table with a smoking service on it. Near it an easychair and a lounge. Cocoanut mats lie before the fireplace, beside the lounge and before the doors. The floor is of stained planking. The double doors at the back and the folding doors at the right have lace curtains, which are drawn halfway. The lower sash of the window is lifted and the window is hung with heavy green plush curtains. The blind is pulled down to the edge of the lifted lower sash. It is a warm afternoon in June and the room is filled with soft sunlight which is waning.

[BRIGID *and* BEATRICE JUSTICE *come in by the door on the left.* BRIGID *is an elderly woman, lowsized, with irongrey hair.* BEATRICE JUSTICE *is a slender dark young woman of 27 years. She wears a wellmade navyblue costume and an elegant simply trimmed black straw hat, and carries a small portfolioshaped handbag.*]

BRIGID

The mistress and Master Archie is at the bath. They never expected you. Did you send word you were back, Miss Justice?

BEATRICE

No. I arrived just now.

BRIGID

[*Points to the easychair.*] Sit down and I tell the Master you are here. Were you long in the train?

BEATRICE

[*Sitting down.*] Since morning.

BRIGID

Master Archie got your postcard with the views of Youghal. You're tired out, I'm sure.

BEATRICE

O, no. [*She coughs rather nervously.*] Did he practise the piano while I was away?

BRIGID

[*Laughs heartily.*] Practise, how are you! Is it Master Archie? He is mad after the milkman's horse now. Had you nice weather down there, Miss Justice?

Document 15:
Title page and the first two pages of the text of *Exiles,* 1918.

Joyce wrote only one surviving play *Exiles,* which he began in 1914 and completed the following year. It was published in London in 1918 by Grant Richards who had eventually published *Dubliners.* The play, in the Ibsen style, was generally considered interesting to read but difficult to produce on stage; it was felt that the dialogue would not enable the actors to convey the essential relationships of the characters. Joyce tried hard to get the play produced and eventually it was first performed in Munich in 1919. However between then and 1950 there were only nine reported productions, including one at the Gaiety Theatre, Dublin, in 1948; an extract from the *Irish Times* review of the Gaiety performance is given below.

Joyce moved to neutral Switzerland in 1915 and he wrote the greater part of *Exiles* there. The photograph below shows him in Zurich in 1919. *(University of Buffalo Library)*

GAIETY THEATRE
" EXILES "

"Exiles" emphasises two aspects of Joyce; his amazing facility in imitating—parodying, if you will—other men's work (in this case he is Joyce-Ibsen) and his Stephen Daedalus-Leopold Bloom obsession with the theme of the dead, unforgiving mother and the wife of questionable fidelity.

Richard Rowan, the central character of "Exiles," is a blood brother of Stephen Daedalus, who returns to Ireland after his mother's death, with Bertha, the woman with whom he has been living in exile, and whom, in his rebellion against established convention, he will not marry.

The unreality of the two major women's parts in this play reinforces a personal theory that Joyce was unsure of himself in handling women of the middle classes. Milly Bloom and Brigid, the servant in "Exiles," come alive; Bertha and Beatrice do not.

As to the presentation, "Exiles" calls for the subtlety and experience of an Edwards-MacLiammoir production; and is considerably beyond the reach of the 'prentice producer and actors of the Sunday Theatre.

(19 Jan. 1948)   K.

I

Once upon a time and a very good time it was there was a moo-cow coming down along the road and this moo-cow that was coming down along the road met a nicens little boy named baby tuckoo......

His father told him that story: his father looked at him through a glass: he had a hairy face.

He was baby tuckoo. The moo-cow came down the road where Betty Byrne lived: she sold lemon platt.

<u>O, the wild rose blossoms
On the little green place</u>

He sang that song. That was his song.

<u>O, the geen wothe botheth</u>

When you wet the bed first it is warm then it gets cold. His mother put on the oilsheet. That had the queer smell.

His mother had a nicer

Document 14:
Page 1 of the final manuscript of *A Portrait of the Artist as a Young Man. (National Library Ms. 920)*

In a single day, 7 January 1904, Joyce wrote an autobiographical story entitled 'A Portrait of the Artist'. He submitted it to the new Dublin literary periodical *Dana* but it was rejected. At once he proceeded to expand it into a long work to be called *Stephen Hero,* a title based on the name of the central figure of the story, Stephen Dedalus — Joyce's pseudonym. In 1907 when *Stephen Hero* was almost finished he decided to rewrite it in a shorter form and call it *A Portrait of the Artist as a Young Man.* When some chapters of this new version were written he threw the manuscript into the fire in a fit of despair over his problems with publishing *Dubliners.* Fortunately his sister Eileen, who was staying with him in Trieste at the time, rescued it. Eventually it was published in serial form by Harriet Weaver in the London periodical the *Egoist* in 1914-15. An American publisher B. W. Huebsch, who had been impressed by *Dubliners,* now read *A Portrait* and arranged to publish it in New York in December 1916.

Harriet Weaver whose photograph appears below became an extremely generous patron of Joyce and subsidised his work by giving him large sums of money for several years. In gratitude Joyce gave her the final manuscript of *A Portrait* and she donated it to the National Library in 1951. The manuscript has dedications by Joyce and Harriet Weaver which are reproduced below.

GAS FROM A BURNER.

Ladies and gents, you are here assembled
To hear why earth and heaven trembled
Because of the black and sinister arts
Of an Irish writer in foreign parts.
He sent me a book ten years ago
I read it a hundred times or so,
Backwards and forwards, down and up,
Through both the ends of a telescope.
I printed it all to the very last word
But by the mercy of the Lord
The darkness of my mind was rent
And I saw the writer's foul intent.
But I owe a duty to Ireland:
I hold her honour in my hand,
This lovely land that always sent
Her writers and artists to banishment
And in a spirit of Irish fun
Betrayed her own leaders, one by one.
'Twas Irish humour, wet and dry,
Flung quicklime into Parnell's eye;
'Tis Irish brains that save from doom
The leaky barge of the Bishop of Rome
For everyone knows the Pope can't belch
Without the consent of Billy Walsh.
O Ireland my first and only love
Where Christ and Caesar are hand and glove!
O lovely land where the shamrock grows!
(Allow me, ladies, to blow my nose)
To show you for strictures I don't care a button
I printed the poems of Mountainy Mutton
And a play he wrote (you've read it, I'm sure)
Where they talk of „bastard" „bugger" and „whore"
And a play on the Word and Holy Paul
And some woman's legs that I can't recall
Written by Moore, a genuine gent
That lives on his property's ten per cent:

* * * * * * * *

I printed folklore from North and South
By Gregory of the Golden Mouth:
I printed poets, sad, silly and solemn:
I printed Patrick What - do - you - Colm:
I printed the great John Milicent Synge
Who soars above on an angel's wing
In the playboy shift that he pinched as swag
From Maunsel's manager's travelling - bag.
But I draw the line at that bloody fellow,
That was over here dressed in Austrian yellow,
Spouting Italian by the hour
To O'Leary Curtis and John Wyse Power
And writing of Dublin, dirty and dear,
In a manner no blackamoor printer could bear.
Shite and onions! Do you think I'll print
The name of the Wellington Monument,
Sydney Parade and the Sandymount tram.
Downes's cakeshop and Williams's jam?
I'm damned if I do — I'm damned to blazes!
Talk about *Irish Names of Places!*
Its a wonder to me, upon my soul,
He forgot to mention Curly's Hole.
No, ladies, my press shall have no share in
So gross a libel on Stepmother Erin.
I pity the poor — that's why I took
A red - headed Scotchman to keep my book.
Poor sister Scotland! Her doom is fell;
She cannot find any more Stuarts to sell.
My conscience is fine as Chinese silk:
My heart is as soft as buttermilk.
Colm can tell you I made a rebate
Of one hundred pounds on the estimate
I gave him for his Irish Review.
I love my country — by herrings I do!
I wish you could see what tears I weep
When I think of the emigrant train and ship.
That's why I publish far and wide
My quite illegible railway guide.
In the porch of my printing institute
The poor and deserving prostitute
Plays every night at catch - as - catch - can
With her tight - breeched British artilleryman
And the foreigner learns the gift of the gab
From the drunken draggletail Dublin drab.
Who was it said: Resist not evil?
I'll burn that book, so help me devil.
I'll sing a psalm as I watch it burn
And the ashes I'll keep in a one - handled urn.
I'll penance do with farts and groans
Kneeling upon my marrowbones.
This very next lent I will unbare
My penitent buttocks to the air
And sobbing beside my printing press
My awful sin I will confess.
My Irish foreman from Bannockburn
Shall dip his right hand in the urn
And sign crisscross with reverent thumb
Memento homo upon my bum.

James Joyce.

Flushing, September 1912.

Document 13:
Extracts from 'Gas from a Burner', Trieste, 1912.

From 1905 onwards Joyce made several attempts to get a publisher to bring out his collection of short stories *Dubliners*. He was unsuccessful as both publishers and printers feared that words and passages in the stories could render them liable to prosecution. Eventually the Dublin publisher Maunsel & Co. accepted the manuscript; an advertisement from their catalogue is reproduced below. The firm of John Falconer was contracted to do the printing and in July 1910 an edition of 1,000 copies was printed. However, at that late stage both the printer and the head of Maunsel & Co., George Roberts, had second thoughts about *Dubliners*. After prolonged negotiations with Joyce, Falconer suddenly destroyed the printed copies in September 1912. Joyce claimed that the books were burnt while Roberts maintained they were guillotined and pulped.

Joyce had come to Dublin to get his books released and after they were destroyed he began 'Gas from a Burner' at Flushing in Holland while waiting for a train to take him back to Trieste where he was then teaching. The lines are presented as being spoken by Roberts ('The Burner') or perhaps by a composite of the publisher and the printer. Joyce had the poem printed as a broadsheet in Trieste and sent most of the copies to his brother Charles to distribute in Dublin.

New Irish Books
Ready or to appear shortly

DUBLINERS. By J. Joyce. Crown 8vo, cloth. 3s. 6d. net (24th Nov.)

A book of studies of Dublin life, which, although detached, is by no means a mere collection of sketches, but has a very distinct unity. Never before has this side of Dublin life been presented in quite so real a manner. The author's style at once removes the book from the category of ordinary fiction and makes it the piece of literature that will no doubt win the same recognition from discerning critics as did his book of poems published a few years ago, of which Mr. Arthur Symons wrote: " . . . so singularly good, so fine and delicate, and yet so full of music and suggestion, that I can hardly choose among them . . . to do such tiny evanescent things . . . is to evoke, not only roses in mid-winter, but the very dew on the roses. Sometimes we are reminded of Elizabethan, more often of Jacobean lyrics."

MAUNSEL & CO., LIMITED
96 Middle Abbey Street, Dublin.

XXXI

O, it was out by Donnycarney
    When the bat flew from tree to tree
My love and I did walk together;
    And sweet were the words she said to me.

Along with us the summer wind
    Went murmuring—O, happily!—
But softer than the breath of summer
    Was the kiss she gave to me.

Document 12:
Printed text, manuscript and musical setting of the poem, 'O, it was out by Donnycarney', published in *Chamber Music*, 1907.

In the period 1901-1904 Joyce wrote a number of poems which he wished to have published as a volume entitled *Chamber Music*. Four publishers rejected the manuscript but Elkin Mathews brought it out in 1907 and there were a number of subsequent editions. The volume consisted of thirty-six poems, of which a number had already appeared in various publications. The first edition consisted of 509 copies and the price was one shilling and sixpence. Joyce claimed that his contract entitled him to royalties after the sale of the first 300 copies but he did not receive any.

The poem, 'O, it was out by Donnycarney', was intended for singing as were many of the other poems in *Chamber Music*. Joyce regarded it as one of his favourites. There are a number of manuscripts of it in his hand but they seem to have been written after he had established its final form and no drafts survive. The manuscript reproduced here is in Yale University Library —James Joyce Manuscripts (1905-27).

The poem has been set to music by a number of composers. The setting from which an extract is given here is by the Irish musician Geoffrey Molyneux Palmer. It is in manuscript form and is reproduced from an item in National Library Ms. 8634.

THE HOLY OFFICE.

Myself unto myself will give
This name Katharsis-Purgative.
I, who dishevelled ways forsook
To hold the poets' grammar-book,
Bringing to tavern and to brothel
The mind of witty Aristotle,
Lest bards in the attempt should err
Must here be my interpreter:
Wherefore receive now from my lip
Peripatetic scholarship.
To enter heaven, travel hell,
Be piteous or terrible
One positively needs the ease,
Of plenary indulgences.
For every true-born mysticist
A Dante is, unprejudiced,
Who safe at ingle-nook, by proxy,
Hazards extremes of heterodoxy
Like him who finds a joy at table,
Pondering the uncomfortable.
Ruling one's life by common sense
How can one fail to be intense?
But I must not accounted be
One of that mumming company —
With him who hies him to appease
His giddy dames' frivolities
While they console him when he whinges
With gold-embroidered Celtic fringes —
Or him who sober all the day
Mixes a naggin in his play —
Or him who conduct „seems to own",
His preference for a man of „tone" —
Or him who plays the rugged patch
To millionaires in Hazelhatch
But weeping after holy fast
Confesses all his pagan past —
Or him who will his hat unfix
Neither to malt nor crucifix
But show to all that poor-dressed be
His high Castilian courtesy —
Or him who loves his Master dear —
Or him who drinks his pint in fear —
Or him who once when snug abed
Saw Jesus Christ without his head
And tried so hard to win for us
The long-lost works of Eschylus.
But all these men of whom I speak
Make me the sewer of their clique.
That they may dream their dreamy dreams
I carry off their filthy streams
For I can do those things for them
Through which I lost my diadem,
Those things for which Grandmother Church
Left me severely in the lurch.
Thus I relieve their timid arses,
Perform my office of Katharsis.
My scarlet leaves them white as wool
Through me they purge a bellyful.
To sister mummers one and all
I act as vicar-general
And for each maiden, shy and nervous,
I do a similar kind service.
For I detect without surprise
That shadowy beauty in her eyes,
The „dare not" of sweet maidenhood
That answers my corruptive „would".
Whenever publicly we meet
She never seems to think of it;
At night when close in bed she lies
And feels my hand between her thighs
My little love in light attire
Knows the soft flame that is desire.
But Mammon places under ban
The uses of Leviathan
And that high spirit ever wars
On Mammon's countless servitors
Nor can they ever be exempt
From his taxation of contempt.
So distantly I turn to view
The shamblings of that motley crew,
Those souls that hate the strength that
[mine has
Steeled in the school of old Aquinas.
Where they have crouched and crawled and
[prayed
I stand the self-doomed, unafraid,
Unfellowed, friendless and alone,
Indifferent as the herring-bone,
Firm as the mountain-ridges where
I flash my antlers on the air.
Let them continue as is meet
To adequate the balance-sheet.
Though they may labour to the grave
My spirit shall they never have
Nor make my soul with theirs at one
Till the Mahamanvantara be done:
And though they spurn me from their door
My soul shall spurn them evermore.

James A. Joyce.

Document 11:
The broadside 'The Holy Office', Pola, 1904–1905.

During the summer and autumn of 1904 Joyce was thinking of going abroad again and supporting himself by teaching while he followed his vocation of writer. He despised the writers of the Irish Literary Revival and as a parting shot he satirised them in 'The Holy Office'. It ridicules the leaders of the Revival, among them Yeats who, it suggests, is controlled by women; Synge writes of drinking while himself always sober; Oliver St. John Gogarty is a snob; Padraic Colum a chameleon; the publisher George Roberts is suggested to be an idolator of George Russell; James S. Starkey is a mouse and George Russell a fool. Joyce portrays his fellow writers as minions of Mammon while he regards himself as Leviathan, to him the spirit of freedom and strength.

Joyce left Dublin with Nora Barnacle on 9 October 1904 and after some weeks secured a post teaching English at the Berlitz School at Pola in Yugoslavia. Before leaving Dublin he left 'The Holy Office' with a printer but did not have the money to pay for the work. When he was settled in at Pola he had it printed there late in 1904 or early in 1905.

Below is a photograph of the Berlitz School at Pola in 1904 — at the right of the Roman arch of Sergius — and an announcement of Joyce's appointment as a teacher at the school.

OUR WEEKLY STORY.

EVELINE.
By Stephen Dædalus.

She sat at the window watching the evening invade the avenue. Her head was leaned against the window-curtain, and in her nostrils was the odour of dusty cretonne. She was tired. Few people passed. The man out of the last house passed on his way home; she heard his footsteps clacking along the concrete pavement, and afterwards crunching on the cinder path before the new red houses. One time there used to be a field there, in which they used to play in the evening with other people's children. Then a man from Belfast bought the field and built houses in it—not like their little brown houses, but bright brick houses, with shining roofs. The children of the avenue used to play together in that field—the Devines, the Waters, the Dunns, little Keogh, the cripple, she and her brothers and sisters. Ernest, however, never played; he was too grown-up. Her father used often to hunt them in out of the field with his blackthorn stick, but usually little Keogh used to keep "nix," and call out when he saw her father coming. Still they seemed to have been rather happy then. Her father was not so bad then, and besides her mother was alive. That was a long time ago; she and her brothers and sisters were all grown up; her mother was dead; Mrs. Dunn was dead, too, and the Waters had gone back to England. Everything changes; now she was going to go away, to leave her home.

Home! She looked round the room, passing in review all its familiar objects. How many times she had dusted it, once a week at least. It was the "best" room, but it seemed to secrete dust everywhere. She had known the room for ten years —more—twelve years, and knew everything in it. Now she was going away. And yet during all those years she had never found out the name of the Australian priest whose yellowing photograph hung on the wall, just above the broken harmonium. He had been a friend of her father's—a school friend. When he showed the photograph to a friend, her father used to pass it with a casual word, "In Australia now—Melbourne."

She had consented to go away—to leave her home. Was it wise—was it honourable? She tried to weigh each side of the question in her mind. In her home at least she had shelter and food; she had those whom she had known all her life about her. She had to work of course both in the house and at business. What would they think of her in the Stores when they discovered she had gone away? Think her a fool, perhaps, and fill up her place by advertisement. Miss Gavan would probably be glad. She, too, would not be sorry to be out of Miss Gavan's clutches. Miss Gavan had an "edge" on her, and used her superior position mercilessly, particularly whenever there were people listening. It was—" Miss Hill, will you please attend to these ladies?" "A little bit smarter, Miss Hill, if you please." She would not cry many tears at leaving the Stores. In her new home in a distant, unknown country, surely she would be free from such indignities! She would then be a married woman—she, Eveline. She would be treated with respect. She would not be treated as her mother had been treated. Even now—at her age, she was over nineteen—she sometimes felt herself in danger of her father's violence. Latterly he had begun to threaten her, saying what he would do were it not for her dead mother's sake. And now she had nobody to protect her. Ernest was dead, and Harry, who was in the church-decorating business, was nearly always down somewhere in the country. Besides, the invariable squabble for money on Saturday night had begun to weary her unspeakably. She always gave her entire wages—seven shillings—and Harry always sent up what he could, but the trouble was to get any money from her father. He said she used to squander the money, that she had no head, that he wasn't going to give her his hard-earned money to throw about the streets, and much more, for he was usually fairly bad on Saturday night. In the end he would give her the money, and ask her had she any intention of buying Sunday's dinner. Then she had to rush out as quickly as she could and do her marketing, holding her black leather purse tightly in her hand as she elbowed her way through the crowds, and returning home late under her load of provisions. She had hard work to keep the house together, and to see that the two young children who had been left to her charge went to school regularly and got their meals regularly. It was hard work—a hard life—but now that she was about to leave it she did not find it a wholly undesirable life.

She was about to explore another life with Frank. Frank was very kind, manly, open-hearted. She was to go away with him by the night boat to be his wife, and to live with him in Buenos Ayres, where he had a home waiting for her. How well she remembered the first time she had seen him (he was lodging in a house on the main road where she used to visit). A few weeks ago it seemed. He was standing at the gate, his peaked cap pushed back on his head, and his hair tumbled forward over a face of bronze. Then they had come to know each other. He used to meet her outside the Stores every evening, and see her home. He took her to see the "Bohemian Girl," and she felt elated as she sat in an unaccustomed part of the theatre with him. He was very fond of music, and sang a little. People knew that they were courting, and when Frank sang about the lass that loves a sailor she always felt pleasantly confused. He used to call her "Poppens" out of fun. First it had been an excitement for her to have a young man, and then she had begun to like him. He had tales of distant countries. He had started as a deck boy at a pound a month on a ship of the Allan line going out to Canada. He told her the names of the ships he had been on, and the names of the different services. He had sailed through the Straits of Magellan, and he told her stories of the terrible Patagonians. He had fallen on his feet in Buenos Ayres, he said, and had come over to the old country just for a holiday. Of course, her father had found out the affair, and had forbidden her to have anything to do with him. " I know these sailor fellows," her father said. Frank and her father had quarrelled one day, and after that she had to meet her lover secretly.

The evening deepened in the avenue. The white of two letters lying in her lap grew indistinct. One was to Harry, the other was to her father. Ernest had been her favourite, but she liked Harry, too. Her father was becoming old lately, she noticed; he would miss her. Sometimes he could be very nice. Not long before, when she had been laid up for a day, he had read her out a ghost-story, and had made toast for her at the fire. Another day, when her mother was alive, they had all gone for a picnic to the Hill of Howth. She remembered her father putting on her mother's bonnet to make the children laugh.

Her time was running out, but she continued to sit by the window, leaning her head against the window-curtain, inhaling the odour of dusty cretonne. Down far in the avenue she could hear a street organ playing. She knew the air. Strange that it should come that very night to remind her of her promise to her mother, her promise to keep the home together as long as she could. She remembered the last night of her mother's illness; she was again in the close, dark room at the other side of the hall, and outside she heard a melancholy air of Italy. The organ-player had been ordered to go away, and given sixpence. She remembered her father strutting back into the sick room, saying: "Damned Italians! coming over here." As she mused, the pitiful vision of her mother's life laid its spell on the very quick of her being—that life of commonplace sacrifices closing in final craziness. She trembled as she heard again her mother's voice saying constantly with foolish insistence: "Derevaun Seraun," "Derevaun Seraun."

She stood up in a sudden impulse of terror. Escape? She must escape! Frank would save her. He could give her life, perhaps love, too. But she wanted life. Why should she be unhappy? She had a right to happiness. Frank would take her in his arms, fold her in his arms. He would save her.

She stood among the swaying crowd in the station at the North Wall. He held her hand and she knew that he was speaking to her, saying something about the passage over and over again. The station was full of soldiers with brown baggages. Through the wide door she caught a glimpse of the black mass of the boat lying in beside the quay wall, with illumined portholes. She answered nothing. She felt her cheek pale and cold, and out of a maze of distress she prayed to God to direct her, to show her what was her duty. The boat blew a long, mournful whistle into the mist. If she went to-morrow she would be on the sea with Frank, steaming towards Buenos Ayres. Their passage had been booked. Could she still draw back, after all he had done for her? Her distress awoke a nausea in her body, and she kept moving her lips in silent, fervent prayer.

A bell clanged upon her heart. She felt him seize her hand. "Come!"

All the seas of the world tumbled about her heart. He was drawing her into them; he would drown her. She gripped with both hands at the iron railing.

"Come!"

No! No! No! It was impossible. Her hands clutched the iron in frenzy. Amid the seas she sent a cry of anguish.

"Eveline! Evvy!"

He rushed beyond the barrier and called to her to follow. He was shouted at to go on, but he still called to her. She set her white face to him, passive, like a helpless animal. Her eyes gave him no sign of love, or farewell or recognition.

Document 10:
The short story 'Eveline', *Irish Homestead,* 10 Sept. 1904.

In July 1904 George Russell invited Joyce to write a story suitable for the farming periodical *Irish Homestead.* He promised a pound as payment and continued: 'It is easy earned money if you can write fluently and don't mind playing to the common understanding and liking once in a way. You can sign any name you like as a pseudonym'. Joyce wrote three stories for the magazine, of which 'Eveline' was the second. He planned to write others but was asked not to submit any more as there were too many letters of complaint from readers. Joyce was ashamed of publishing his work in what was popularly known as 'the pigs' paper' and he signed the stories 'Stephen Daedalus'. These three stories were the earliest of the fifteen eventually published in the collection *Dubliners* in 1914.

Joyce had a very good tenor voice and around the time he was writing for the *Irish Homestead* he wondered whether he should choose singing or writing as a career. In May 1904 he won the bronze medal at the Feis Ceoil and he was invited to perform in a concert which featured John McCormack during Horse Show week that year.

The notices below are from the *Freeman's Journal,* August 1904.

**ANTIENT CONCERT ROOMS.
EXHIBITION OF IRISH
INDUSTRIES
AND
GRAND IRISH CONCERT,
THIS (SATURDAY) EVENING,**
At 8 o'clock.
Artistes:—
Miss AGNES TREACY,
Miss OLIVE BARRY,
Madame HALL
Miss WALKER (Marie Nic Shiubhlaigh).
Mr. J. C. DOYLE,
Mr. JAMES A. JOYCE, and
Mr. J. F. M'CORMACK.
Orchestra conducted by
Miss EILEEN REIDY, A.L.C.M., R.I.A.M.
Prices—3s, 2s, and 1s.

SATURDAY NIGHT'S CONCERT.

A concert was given in the large hall of the Antient Concert Rooms on Saturday night, and attracted a full house. The programme was a first-rate one. The Exhibition String Band played selections of Irish melodies and of operatic music of Irish composers. Mr. J. C. Doyle sang a number of songs in first-rate style. His voice is full, sweet, of considerable range, and with uncommon capability of expression. His singing is characterised by remarkable intelligence and whether in the light playful mood of the peasant ballad, the sentimental ditty, or the strength and passion of the war song, he was fully equal to the occasion. He was encored at every song. Miss Agnes Treacy sang charmingly a number of Irish airs in Gaelic and English, and was rewarded with hearty applause and imperative encores. Mr. James A. Joyce, the possessor of a sweet tenor voice, sang charmingly "The Sally Gardens," and gave a pathetic rendering of "The Croppy Boy." Madame Halle gave a Miss Maire Nic Shiubhlaigh is a lady of considerable histrionic talent, and her selection for recitation gave an opportunity for the display of her powers in narrative, the pathetic and the impassioned, all of which she realised fully. She was not so successful in a recitative rendering of one of Mr. Yeats' poems, whether due to nervousness at the novelty of the form, or that this style is not so well within her gifts, as the natural delivery in which she excelled. She was vociferously applauded. Mr. J. F. M'Cormack was the hero of the evening. It was announced as his last public appearance in Ireland, and the evident feeling of the audience at the parting, seemed to unnerve him a good deal. His voice is one of great resonance, as well as of high range, and his powerful notes were heard in a varied selection of Irish melodies. The audience seemed as if it would never hear and see enough of him, and twice he had to respond to triple encores, while he was recalled times almost without number.

Leinster Street
16th August 1904

My Dearest

My loneliness which I have so deeply felt, since we parted last night seemed to fade away as if by magic. but. alas. it was only for a short time. and I then became worse than ever, when I read your letter from the moment that I close my eyes till I open them again in the morning. It seems to me that I am always in your company. under every possible variety of circumstances talking to you walking with you meeting you suddenly in different places until I am beginning to wonder if my spirit takes leave of my body in sleep and goes to seek you, and what is more find you or perhaps this is nothing but a fantasy. Occasionally too I fall into a fit of melancholy that lasts for the day and which I find almost impossible to dispel it is about time now I think that I should finish this letter as the more I write the lonelier I feel in consequence of you being so far away and the thought of having to write write what I would wish to speak were you beside me makes me feel utterly miserable so with best wishes and love I now close

Believe me to be ever Yours
Norah Barnacle

Document 9:
Letter of Nora Barnacle to Joyce, 16 August 1904. *(Cornell University Library)*

Following their meeting on 16 June Joyce and Nora Barnacle met regularly and exchanged a number of letters. Joyce suspected that this letter of 16 August was not entirely spontaneous and that Nora had copied at least part of it from somewhere. She admitted this and promised to write more naturally in future. In the event Nora's letters were to become one of the sources for the famous monologue of Molly Bloom that ends *Ulysses*.

The well known photograph below dates from that summer when Joyce, then age 22, was walking out with Nora Barnacle, and it shows the yachting cap he was wearing the day they met. It was taken by Constantine P. Curran, a contemporary of Joyce at University College, who is one of the group shown in Document 4. Asked what he was thinking about while being photographed Joyce replied, 'I was wondering would he lend me five shillings'. *(University College Dublin Library, C.P. Curran Papers)*

> 60 Shelbourne Road
>
> I may be blind. I looked for a long time at a head of reddish-brown hair and decided it was not yours. I went home quite dejected. I would like to make an appointment but it might not suit you. I hope you will be kind enough to make one with me — if you have not forgotten me!
>
> 15 June 1904 James A Joyce

Document 8:
Post-card from Joyce to Nora Barnacle, 15 June 1904. *(Cornell University Library)*

Joyce met Nora Barnacle in Nassau Street on 10 June 1904. Nora was from Galway and was then working in Finn's Hotel, 1 & 2 Leinster Street, a street which is a continuation of Nassau Street. Joyce was wearing a yachting cap and she took him for a sailor; with his penetrating blue eyes she thought he might be Swedish. They made a date for the Westland Row corner of Merrion Square for the evening of 14 June but Nora failed to appear. Joyce wrote her this note and another appointment was made. On that occasion Nora did turn up and the pair went walking at Ringsend. The date was 16 June 1904, a day later immortalised by Joyce as Bloomsday.

The photograph of Nora shows her when she was living in Galway before she came to Dublin. The photograph below (National Library, Lawrence Collection N.S. 5398) shows Nassau Street as it was in the period when Joyce and Nora met; indeed there is a possibility, albeit slight, that one or both of them are among the passers-by.

THE MOTOR DERBY

INTERVIEW WITH THE FRENCH CHAMPION.

(FROM A CORRESPONDENT.)

PARIS, SUNDAY.

In the Rue d'Anjou, not far from the Church of the Madeleine, is M. Henri Fournier's place of business. "Paris-Automobile"—a company of which M. Fournier is the manager—has its headquarters there. Inside the gateway is a big square court, roofed over, and on the floor of the court and on great shelves extending from the floor to the roof are ranged motor-cars of all sizes, shapes, and colours. In the afternoon this court is full of noises—the voices of workmen, the voices of buyers talking in half-a-dozen languages, the ringing of telephone bells, the horns sounded by the "chauffeurs" as the cars come in and go out—and it is almost impossible to see M. Fournier unless one is prepared to wait two or three hours for one's turn. But the buyers of "autos" are, in one sense, people of leisure. The morning, however, is more favourable, and yesterday morning, after two failures, I succeeded in seeing M. Fournier.

M. Fournier is a slim, active-looking young man, with dark reddish hair. Early as the hour was our interview was now and again broken in upon by the importunate telephone.

"You are one of the competitors for the Gordon-Bennett Cup, M. Fournier?"

"Yes, I am one of three selected to represent France."

"And you are also a competitor, are you not, for the Madrid Prize?"

"Yes."

"Which of the races comes first—the Irish race or the Madrid race?"

"The Madrid race. It takes place early in May, while the race for the International Cup does not take place till July."

"I suppose you are preparing actively for your races?"

"Well, I have just returned from a tour to Monte Carlo and Nice."

"On your racing machine?"

"No, on a machine of smaller power."

"Have you determined what machine you will ride in the Irish race?"

"Practically."

"May I ask the name of it—is it a Mercédes?"

"No, a Mors."

"And its horse-power?"

"Eighty."

"And on this machine you can travel at a rate of——?"

"You mean its highest speed?"

"Yes."

"Its highest speed would be a hundred and forty kilometres an hour."

"But you will not go at that rate all the time during the race?"

"Oh, no. Of course its average speed for the race would be lower than that."

"An average speed of how much?"

"Its average speed would be a hundred kilometres an hour, perhaps a little more than that, something between a hundred and a hundred and ten kilometres an hour."

"A kilometre is about a half-mile, is it not?"

"More than that, I should think. There are how many yards in your mile?"

"Seventeen hundred and sixty, if I am right."

"Then your half-mile has eight hundred and eighty yards. Our kilometre is just equal to eleven hundred yards."

"Let me see. Then your top speed is nearly eighty-six miles an hour, and your average speed is sixty-one miles an hour?"

"I suppose so, if we calculate properly."

"It is an appalling pace! It is enough to burn our roads. I suppose you have seen the roads you are to travel?"

"No."

"No! You don't know the course, then?"

"I know it slightly. I know it, that is, from some sketches that were given of it in the Paris newspapers."

"But, surely, you will want a better knowledge than that?"

"Oh, certainly. In fact, before the month is over, I intend to go to Ireland to inspect the course. Perhaps I shall go in three weeks' time."

"Will you remain any time in Ireland?"

"After the race?"

"Yes."

"I am afraid not. I should like to, but I don't think I can."

"I suppose you would not like to be asked your opinion of the result?"

"Hardly."

"Yet, which nation do you fear most?"

"I fear them all—Germans, Americans, and English. They are all to be feared."

"And how about Mr. Edge?"

No answer.

"He won the prize the last time, did he not?"

"O, yes."

"Then he should be your most formidable opponent?"

"O, yes . . . But, you see, Mr. Edge won, of course, but . . . a man who was last of all, and had no chance of winning might win if the other machines broke."

Whatever way one looks at this statement it appears difficult to challenge its truth.

Document 7:
Report of an interview by Joyce with the French racing driver Henri Fournier, *Irish Times*, 7 April 1903.

When Joyce was studying medicine in Paris he was able to earn some money writing reviews for the *Daily Express* due to the influence of Lady Gregory. He also did an interview with the French driver Fournier for the *Irish Times*. His brother Stanislaus later wrote of the circumstances as follows:

> 'His last contribution to the Irish newspapers from Paris was an interview for the *Irish Times* of the 5th April with a French motorist, M. Fournier, who was to take part in the race for the Gordon Bennett cup to be run in Ireland in the following July. The interview is ingenuous. My brother does not know what car M. Fournier will drive or whether the Madrid race is before or after the 'Motor Derby', and it is evident from the interview that he knows nothing about motoring and cares, if possible, less'.

The photograph below (from *The Car*, 8 July 1903) shows a scene at the Gordon Bennett race that year. Fournier did not participate after all but Joyce made the occasion the background for his short story 'After the Race', published in December that year in the *Irish Homestead* and afterwards included in the collection *Dubliners*.

Photo. by] COOLING THE TYRES OF BARON DE CATERS' CAR IN THE ATHY CONTROL. [*Lafayette, Dublin*

1902

To LADY GREGORY[1]
N.D. [November 1902]   *7 St Peter's Terrace, Cabra, Dublin*

Dear Lady Gregory: I have broken off my medical studies here and am going to trouble you with a history. I have a degree of B.A. from the Royal University, and I had made plans to study medicine here. But the college authorities are determined I shall not do so, wishing I dare say to prevent me from securing any position of ease from which I might speak out my heart. To be quite frank I am without means to pay my medical fees and they refuse to get me any grinding or tuitions or examining—alleging inability—although they have done and are doing so for men who were stuck in the exams I passed. I want to get a degree in medicine, for then I can build up my work securely. I want to achieve myself—little or great as I may be—for I know that there is no heresy or no philosophy which is so abhorrent to my church as a human being, and accordingly I am going to Paris. I intend to study medicine at the University of Paris supporting myself there by teaching English. I am going alone and friendless—I know of a man who used to live somewhere near Montmartre but I have never met him—into another country, and I am writing to you to know can you help me in any way. I do not know what will happen to me in Paris but my case can hardly be worse than it is here. I am leaving Dublin by the night boat on Monday 1st December and my train leaves Victoria Station for Newhaven the same night. I am not despondent however because I know that even if I fail to make my way such failure proves very little. I shall try myself against the powers of the world. All things are inconstant except the faith of the soul, which changes all things and fills their inconstancy with light. And though I seem to have been driven out of my country here as a misbeliever I have found no man yet with a faith like mine.

[1] The original of this letter has not been traced. A typewritten copy made by Lady Gregory was found amongst the papers of the late W. B. Yeats. It has an inscription on the back in W. B. Yeats's handwriting and there is of course no question of its authenticity.

Document 6:
Copy of a letter from Joyce to Lady Gregory, c. November 1902 (reproduced from Stuart Gilbert, ed., *Letters of James Joyce*, Faber and Faber, 1957).

Joyce graduated from University College in the summer of 1902. That autumn he began to study medicine at the Catholic University School of Medicine in Cecilia Street which was associated with University College. However in a matter of months he decided to continue his medical studies in Paris. He set out for Paris on 1 December 1902 and this letter to Lady Gregory must have been written shortly before that date.

Below are a cartoon of Lady Gregory by Grace Gifford and a photograph of Joyce in his graduation robes. *(National Library R. 14,363* and *Southern Illinois University Library, Carbondale)*

Document 5:
Extracts from a review by Joyce, 'Ibsen's New Drama', *Fortnightly Review,* 1 April 1900.

Joyce wrote to the editor of the prestigious London periodical, *Fortnightly Review,* offering to contribute a general article on Ibsen. The editor replied that he did not need a general article but might accept a review of Ibsen's latest play *When We Dead Awaken.* The play was not available in an English translation so Joyce read it in French; he later learned Dano-Norwegian so that he could read Ibsen in the original. He promptly wrote a sixteen page review for which he received twelve guineas. This is the earliest surviving publication of a Joyce work — unfortunately no copy is known to exist of 'Et Tu, Healy!', a defence of Parnell written by Joyce when he was aged nine and which his father had printed for distribution to his friends.

Joyce translated two of Gerhart Hauptmann's plays hoping to have them performed by the Irish Literary Theatre. However, in October 1901 he learned that the next plays planned for the Theatre were Douglas Hyde's *Casadh-an-tSugáin* and *Diarmuid and Grania,* adapted by W. B. Yeats and George Moore from, as Joyce put it, 'the broken lights of Irish myth'. Disappointed he wrote an article 'The Day of the Rabblement', attacking the provincialism of the Irish Literary Theatre and submitted it to the College magazine *St. Stephen's* which rejected it. Around the same time *St. Stephen's* also rejected an article by another student, Francis Skeffington, advocating equal status for women at the University. Determined not to be silenced the two went to a printer and had their articles published as an eight page pamphlet with the title *Two Essays.*

THE
FORTNIGHTLY
REVIEW.

EDITED BY W. L. COURTNEY

APRIL, 1900.

		PAGE
I. OUR MILITARY NEEDS	By Major Arthur Griffiths	527
II. FIFTY-EIGHT YEARS, AS CHILD AND WOMAN, IN SOUTH AFRICA	Edited by Maynard Butler	537
III. THE FUTURE OF SOUTH AFRICA	By Wm. Hosken, *Chairman, Uitlander Council*	551
IV. THE HOUSE OF MOLIÈRE	By W. E. Garrett Fisher	557
V. IBSEN'S NEW DRAMA	By James Joyce	575
VI. THE NEXT AGRICULTURAL CENSUS	By William E. Bear	591
VII. GERMANY AS A NAVAL POWER	By Dr. Karl Blind	602
VIII. "WITH BUT AFTER"	By Rollo Appleyard	615
IX. UNCHANGING DOGMA AND CHANGEFUL MAN.	By Wilfrid Ward	628
X. A ROYAL VISIT TO IRELAND	By Michael MacDonagh	649
XI. AN AMERICAN PARALLEL TO THE PRESENT CAMPAIGN.	By Major E. S. Valentine	660
XII. THE CONFEDERATION OF SOUTH AFRICA.	By Edward Dicey, C.B.	668
XIII. THE LATE CAMPAIGN IN NATAL		680
XIV. IONA—Part II.	By Fiona Macleod	692
XV. CORRESPONDENCE— By Herbert Spencer, E. T. Cook, W. A. Baillie-Grohman, Stephen Paget, W. S. Lilly, and Canon Malcolm MacColl.		710

LONDON:
CHAPMAN AND HALL, LIMITED,
11, HENRIETTA STREET, COVENT GARDEN, W.C.

NEW YORK: LEONARD SCOTT PUBLICATION CO.
NEW YORK: THE INTERNATIONAL NEWS CO.   LEIPZIG: BROCKHAUS.
MELBOURNE: GEO. ROBERTSON & CO.   VIENNA: GEROLD & CO.
PARIS: LIBRAIRIE GALIGNANI.   ROTTERDAM: H. A. KRAMERS & SON.
BERLIN: ASHER & CO.   AMSTERDAM: J. G. ROBBERS.
ADELAIDE: W. C. RIGBY.   PRICE 2s. 6d.

Two Essays.

"A Forgotten Aspect of
the University Question"

BY

F. J. C. SKEFFINGTON

AND

BY

JAMES A. JOYCE.

PRICE TWOPENCE.

Printed by
GERRARD BROS.,
37 STEPHEN'S GREEN,
DUBLIN.

IBSEN'S NEW DRAMA.

Twenty years have passed since Henrik Ibsen wrote *A Doll's House*, thereby almost marking an epoch in the history of drama. During those years his name has gone abroad through the length and breadth of two continents, and has provoked more discussion and criticism than that of any other living man. He has been upheld as a religious reformer, a social reformer, a Semitic lover of righteousness, and as a great dramatist. He has been rigorously denounced as a meddlesome intruder, a defective artist, an incomprehensible mystic, and, in the eloquent words of a certain English critic, "a muck-ferreting dog." Through the perplexities of such diverse criticism, the great genius of the man is day by day coming out as a hero comes out amid the earthly trials. The dissonant cries are fainter and more distant, the random praises are rising in steadier and more choral chaunt. Even to the uninterested bystander it must seem significant that the interest attached to this Norwegian has never flagged for over a quarter of a century. It may be questioned whether any man has held so firm an empire over the thinking world in modern times. Not Rousseau; not Emerson; not Carlyle; not any of those giants of whom almost all have passed out of human ken. Ibsen's power over two generations has been enhanced by his own reticence. Seldom, if at all, has he condescended to join battle with his enemies. It would appear as if the storm of fierce debate rarely broke in upon his wonderful calm. The conflicting voices have not influenced his work in the very smallest degree. His output of dramas has been regulated by the utmost order, by a clockwork routine, seldom found in the case of genius. Only once he answered his assailants after their violent attack on *Ghosts*. But from *The Wild Duck* to *John Gabriel Borkman*, his dramas have appeared almost mechanically at intervals of two years. One is apt to overlook the sustained energy which such a plan of campaign demands; but even surprise at this must give way to admiration at the gradual, irresistible advance of this extraordinary man. Eleven plays, all dealing with modern life, have been published. Here is the list: *A Doll's House, Ghosts, An Enemy of the People, The Wild Duck, Rosmersholm, The Lady from the Sea, Hedda Gabler, The Master Builder, Little Eyolf, John Gabriel Borkman,* and lastly—his new drama, published at Copenhagen, December 19th, 1899—*When We Dead Awaken*. This play is already in process of translation into almost a dozen different languages—a fact which speaks volumes for the power of its author. The drama is written in prose, and is in three acts.

* * * * * * * *

the drama to plead for itself. But this at least is clear, that in this play Ibsen has given us nearly the very best of himself. The action is neither hindered by many complexities, as in *The Pillars of Society*, nor harrowing in its simplicity, as in *Ghosts*. We have whimsicality, bordering on extravagance, in the wild Ulfheim, and subtle humour in the sly contempt which Rubek and Maja entertain for each other. But Ibsen has striven to let the drama have perfectly free action. So he has not bestowed his wonted pains on the minor characters. In many of his plays these minor characters are matchless creations. Witness Jacob Engstrand, Tönnesen, and the demonic Molvik! But in this play the minor characters are not allowed to divert our attention.

On the whole, *When We Dead Awaken* may rank with the greatest of the author's work—if, indeed, it be not the greatest. It is described as the last of the series, which began with *A Doll's House*—a grand epilogue to its ten predecessors. Than these dramas, excellent alike in dramaturgic skill, characterisation, and supreme interest, the long roll of drama, ancient or modern, has few things better to show.

JAMES A. JOYCE.

Document 4:
B.A. degree examination results of the Royal University, 1902, reproduced from the *Royal University of Ireland Calendar,* 1903.

University College, at 86 St. Stephen's Green, had begun in the eighteen fifties as the Catholic University with Newman as the first rector. In Joyce's time it was run by the Jesuits. While it did not confer degrees the students could sit for the examinations of the Royal University and get degrees from that institution.

Joyce was a student from 1898 to 1902, taking Modern Languages. He was disappointed with some of the teachers and did not attend lectures regularly. Instead he studied privately and did not confine himself to the set courses. He was particularly interested in contemporary European literature, especially the works of the Norwegian Henrik Ibsen and the German Gerhart Hauptmann.

The photograph below shows Joyce with some of his teachers and contemporaries at University College (National Library R. 15,521). The photograph of University College dates from about 1900 (National Library R. 15,519).

REV. G. O'NEILL, JAS. JOYCE, J. M. O'SULLIVAN, R. J. KINAHAN, JAS CLANDILLON, PATRICK SEMPLE
GEORGE CLANCY, REV. E. HOGAN, S.J., PROF. ED. CADIC, REV. JOS. DARLINGTON
FELIX HACKETT, SEUMAS O'KELLY, MICH. LENNON, CON. P. CURRAN

B.A. DEGREE EXAMINATION (AUTUMN, 1902).

MODERN LITERATURE.

First Class.

Hull, Melissa S., . . . Victoria College, Belfast.
Steinberger, Cecilia L. M. (Sch.), . . . Queen's College, Galway.
Ryan, Mary K., . . . University College and Loreto College, Stephen's-green, Dublin.
Hye, Mary B . . . St. Mary's University College, Dublin.

Second Class.

Hore, Eleanor A. . . . University College, and Loreto College, Stephen's-green, Dublin.
Codd, Brigid M., . . . St. Mary's University College, Dublin.
Spence, Grace W., . . . Victoria College, Belfast.
Worth, Terza, . . . Victoria College, Belfast.
Cleary, Mary E., . . . University College, and Loreto College, Stephen's-green, Dublin.
Gallogly, Michael F., . . St. Colman's College, Newry.
Pyper, Hugh, . . . Private study.
Bennett, Muriel L. M., . . Alexandra College, Dublin, and private study.
Colhoun, Elizabeth J., . . Victoria College, Belfast.
Park, John E., . . . Private study.

PASS.

Anderson, Elizabeth M. J. Loreto College, Stephen's-green, Dublin.
Coffey, Margaret, . . . Alexandra College, Dublin, and private study.
Curran, Constantine P., . University College, Dublin.
Gibson, Mary, . . . Queen's College, Cork.
Gordon, Martha K. B., . Kelvin House, Belfast.
Haughey, Margaret A., . University College, and Loreto College, Stephen's-green, Dublin.
Hickie, Alice, . . . Private tuition.
Horgan, Michael J., . . Queen's College, Cork.
Joyce, James A., . . . University College, Dublin.
Lipsett, Edith D., B MUS. Alexandra College, Dublin.
Lydon, Patrick J., . . Queen's College, Galway.
O'Kelly, James J., . . University College, Dublin.
O'Neill, Edward, . . . Private study.
O'Reilly, Anne B., . . University College, and Loreto College, Stephen's-green, Dublin.
Perry, Ellen O., . . . Alexandra College, Dublin.
Robinson, Eleanor, . . Victoria College, Belfast.
Thorpe, Florence E., . . Victoria College, Belfast.

UNIVERSITY COLLEGE, ST. STEPHEN'S GREEN

Document 3:
Essay, 'Trust Not Appearances', written by Joyce at Belvedere College about 1897. *(Cornell University Library, Joyce Manuscripts I-Ir)*

In Belvedere Joyce was for the most part a well-behaved and pious boy and served two terms as prefect of the Sodality of the Virgin Mary. His devout attitude at that period of his life is indicated by the initials at the beginning and end of the essay: AMDG (*Ad Maiorem Dei Gloriam* – to the greater glory of God) and LDS (*Laus Deo Semper* – may God be ever praised). His aptitude for essay writing was recognised at Belvedere and he won a number of national prizes. Unfortunately this is the only specimen which has survived.

> evil. How beautiful it seems as the harbinger of good and how cruel as the messenger of ill! The man who waits on the temper of a King is but a tiny craft in that great ocean. Thus we see the hollowness of appearances. The hypocrite is the worst kind of villian yet under the appearance of virtue he conceals the worst of vices. The friend, who is but the fane of fortune ~~cringes to the~~ ~~poor~~ & grovells at the feet of wealth. But the man, who has no ambition, no wealth no luxury save Contentment cannot hide the joy of happiness that flows from a clear conscience & an easy mind.
>
> LDS.
>
> *James A. Joyce*

Appearances

Trust not Appearances

There is nothing so deceptive and for that so alluring as a good surface. The sea, when beheld in the noon sun -light of a summer's day, the sky, the air, the faint and amber glimmer of an Autumn sun, are pleasing to the eye; but how different the scene, when the wild anger of the elements has waked again the discord of com- -fusion, how different the ocean's foaming with froth & foam, to the calm, placid sea that just glanced and rippled verily in the sun. But the best examples of the fickleness of appearances are:— Man and Fortune. The cringing, deny- -ing, the high and haughty mien, look, the worthlessness of character, like conceal the worthlessness of the character. Fortune that glittering bauble whose brilliant glimmer

has allured and trifled with both proud and poor, is as wavering as the wind. Still however, there is a "something" that tells us the character of man. It is the eye, the only traitor that even the staunchest will of a fiendish villain cannot overcome. It is the eye that reveals to us the guilt or innocence, the vices or the virtues of the soul. This is the on- -ly exception to the proverb 'Trust not appearances'. In every other case the real worth has to be searched for. The garb of royalty or of dem- -ocracy are but the shadows that a man leaves behind him. "It is an unhappy lot that man, that hangs on princes' favours," the fickle tide of ever changing fortune brings with it—good as

Document 2:
Examination results of the Intermediate Education Board showing Joyce's marks, 1895.

At the age of six and a half Joyce was sent to the Jesuit school, Clongowes Wood College, of which a photograph from the period 1880-1910 appears below (National Library, Lawrence Collection R. 3994). He had to leave at the age of nine because his family could no longer afford it. After a spell at the Christian Brothers' school in North Richmond Street the Jesuits allowed him to complete his education free at Belvedere College. There he sat for the public examinations of the Intermediate Education Board in 1894, 1895, 1897 and 1898, the results of which were published annually by the Board. He was an excellent student and won a number of prizes.

The extract below is from the autobiographical novel *A Portrait of the Artist as a Young Man* (Chap. II) in which Joyce assumes the name Stephen Dedalus.

— I never liked the idea of sending him to the christian brothers myself, said Mrs. Dedalus.
— Christian brothers be damned! said Mr. Dedalus. Is it with Paddy Stink and Mickey Mud? No, let him stick to the jesuits in God's name since he began with them. They'll be of service to him in after years. Those are the fellows that can get you a position.

Intermediate Education Board for Ireland. [Boys, Examinations, 1895

Examination Number	STUDENT'S NAME AND ADDRESS	Greek 1200	Latin 1200	English 1200	Commercial English 400	French 700	Italian 500	Celtic 600	Arithmetic 500	Book-keeping 200	Euclid 600	Algebra 600	Natural Philosophy 500	Chemistry 500	Drawing 500	Shorthand 300	Total under Rule 55	Examination Number
3821	Jones, Christopher F., Merchant Taylors' Sch., Wellington qy., Dublin	×	294	395	35	343	×	×	310	×	185	150	×	×	120	190	2022	3821
3822	[Failed]	×	×	7	×	3	×	f	f	×	f	f	×	×	80	×	90	3822
3823	Jones, James E., Educational Institution, Dundalk	×	f	255	20	568	×	×	330	×	220	10	130	50	170	×	1859	3823
3824	Jones, Sidney F., Avoca School, Blackrock	299	159	200	×	254	×	×	10	×	165	5	×	×	f	×	1092	3824
3825	Jones, Webb B., Portora Royal School, Enniskillen	×	f	185	×	65	×	×	175	×	350	275	×	×	35	×	1085	3825
3826	[Failed]	×	×	50	×	f	×	×	20	P	f	f	f	×	85	×	155	3826
3827	[Failed]	×	f	f	×	21	×	×	145	×	245	30	×	×	25	×	466	3827
3828	Jordan, Hugh, Christian Schools, Newry [P Ex '94]	×	×	225	×	219	×	142	150	×	165	60	100	60	135	×	1442	3828
3829	Joyce, James A., Belvedere College (s.j.), Dublin [P.Ex.'94]	×	636	540	×	410	223	×	250	×	175	175	190	100	×	×	2699	3829
3830	[Failed]	×	f	27	×	×	×	×	f	15	f	f	f	×	×	×	42	3830
3831	[Failed]	×	f	15	×	f	×	×	205	f	50	f	×	×	55	f	325	3831
3832	[Failed]	×	f	25	×	f	×	×	f	×	135	f	×	×	×	×	160	3832
3833	Judge, Maurice J., Blackrock College, co. Dublin	×	f	180	×	57	×	×	10	×	105	f	×	×	×	×	352	3833
3834	Judge, Thomas M., Rockwell College, Cashel	×	174	60	×	221	×	×	110	×	155	f	×	×	×	×	720	3834
3835	Kane, John J., Christian Schools, Tipperary	×	256	240	×	200	×	f	55	×	85	>	×	×	160	×	1136	3835
3836	[Failed]																×	3836
3837	Kavanagh, Jeremiah M., Christian												P	f	f	×	1512	3837
3838	Kavanagh, John J., Christian Sch												×	f	65	×	684	3838
3839	Kavanagh, Patrick, Christian Scho												×	×	f	×	276	3839
3840	Kavanagh, Patrick J., Christian S												×	×	5	×	1276	3840
3841	[Not Examined]												×	×	170	25	×	3841
3842	[Failed]												×	×	15	×	253	3842
3843	Kavanagh, William, Rockwell Coll												×	×	f	×	2051	3843
3844	Kealy, Michael, Christian Schools,												×	×	f	30	365	3844
3845	[Failed]												×	×	5	×	5	3845
3846	Kean, William F., Christian Schoo												210	115	115	×	2335	3846
3847	Keane, Daniel, Christian Schools,												250	400	185	×	3174	3847
3848	[Failed]												×	×	f	f	×	3848
3849	Keane, William, Christian Schools												×	×	30	f	479	3849
3850	Keany, Matthew J., St. Patrick's C												45	×	f	×	774	3850
3851	[Failed]												×	×	f	×	103	3851
3852	Kearney, John, Presentation Colle												×	×	140	×	2279	3852
3853	[Failed]												×	×	105	×	390	3853
3854	[Failed]												×	×	35	×	35	3854
3855	[Failed]												×	×	×	×	175	3855
3856	[Failed]												×	×	f	×	60	3856
3857	[Failed]												×	×	f	×	190	3857
3858	Keeffe, Michael, Christian Schools												30	×	30	×	223	3858

Intermediate Education Board for Ireland.

JUNIOR GRADE.

TABLE I.—EXHIBITIONS, value £20 a-year each, tenable for Three Years, have been awarded to the following Students:—

Order of Merit.	Examination Number.	STUDENT'S NAME AND ADDRESS.	Net Total of Marks under Rule 55
1	3338	Farrell, James A., Presentation Coll., Queenstown [P.Ex. '94]	5212
2	3756	Houston, Robert M., Academical Institution, Coleraine	5016
3	4115	MacMahon, Bernard, Rockwell College, Cashel [P.Ex.'94]	4795
4	4135	M'Cabe, Robert W., Clongowes Wood College (s.j.), Sallins	4614
5	2676	Boyland, Albert H., St. Macarten's Seminary, Monaghan	4583
6	4746	O'Neill, John, Rockwell College, Cashel	4450
7	3787	Hutchinson, John, Clongowes Wood College (s.j.), Sallins	4343
163	4896	Richardson, John J., St. Mel's College, Longford	2701
164	3829	Joyce, James A., Belvedere College (s.j.), Dublin [P.Ex.'94]	2699

Document 1:
Photographs of James Joyce at the age of two, and of James with his parents and maternal grandfather, John Murray.

James Joyce was born in Dublin on 2 February 1882. He was the eldest of fifteen children of whom only ten survived infancy. His father was a clever but spendthrift Corkman, and when his post in the office of the Collector of Rates was abolished in 1892 the family's sinking fortunes forced them to move to ever less fashionable areas of Dublin. This background may help to explain the bitterness and arrogance shown by James when he later came to turn his life's experiences into art.

The photograph of James and his parents was taken when he was six and a half, a few hours before he entered Clongowes Wood College. The photograph below shows the house where he was born, 41 Brighton Square, Rathgar.

The photographs are from Southern Illinois University Library, Carbondale; from an original formerly in the possession of Joyce's sister, Mrs. May Joyce Monaghan; National Library of Ireland R. 16,043.

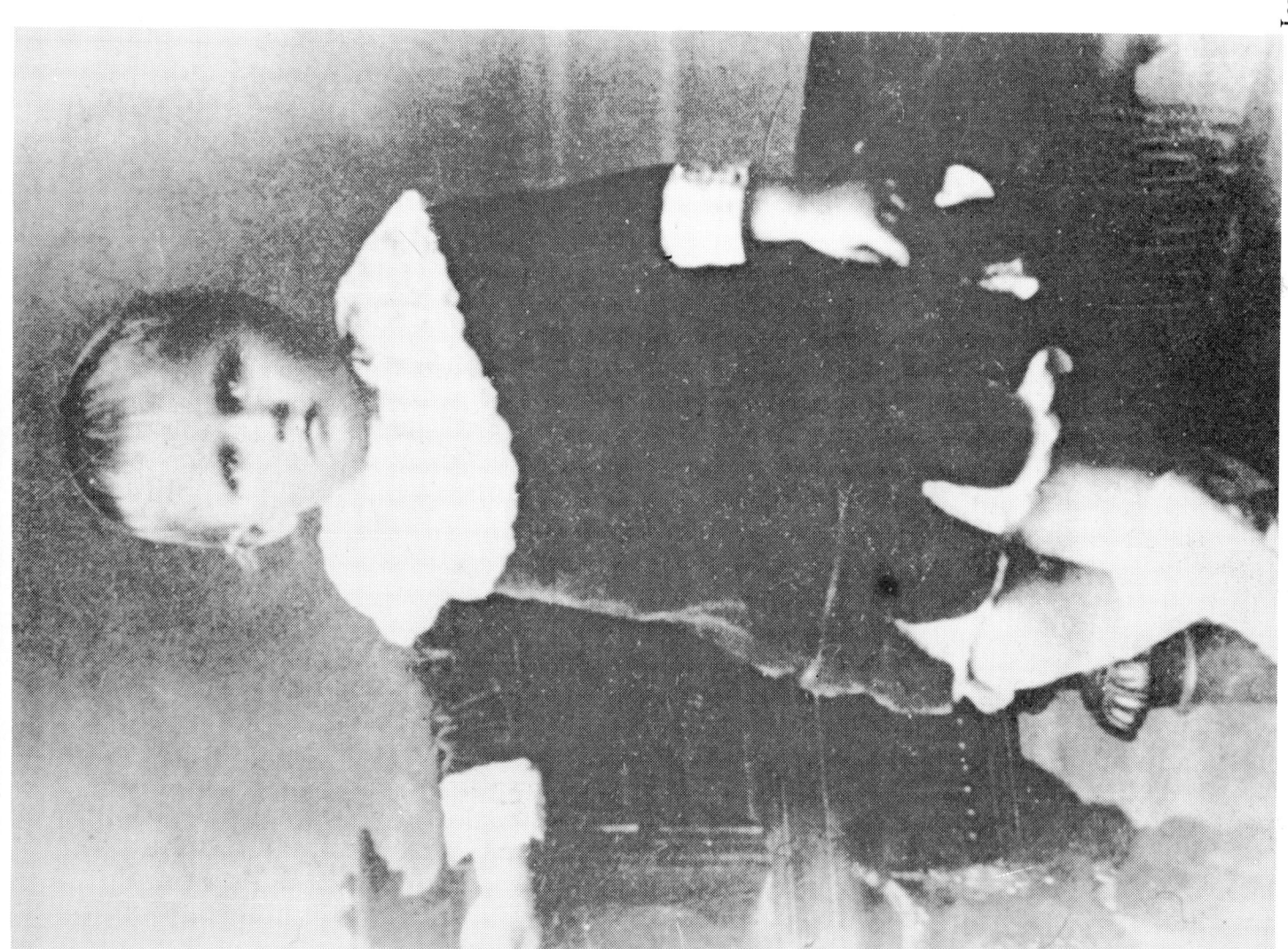

James Joyce with his mother, father, and maternal grandfather (John Murray), taken on the day in September 1888 when he entered Clongowes Wood College

James Joyce as a baby

A JAMES JOYCE CHRONOLOGY

1882   James Augustine Joyce was born on 2 February at 41 Brighton Square, Rathgar, Dublin.

1888   Family moved to Bray; Joyce was enrolled at Clongowes Wood College.

1891   Wrote 'Et Tu, Healy!' (not extant) on the betrayal of Parnell; withdrawn from Clongowes.

1893-98 Studied at Belvedere College.

1898   Enrolled at University College, Dublin.

1900   Published 'Ibsen's New Drama' in the *Fortnightly Review*; wrote 'A Brilliant Career' (a play, not extant).

1901   Published 'The Day of the Rabblement', attacking the Irish Literary Theatre, in the pamphlet *Two Essays*.

1902   Graduated from University College with degree in modern languages.

1903   Studied medicine in Paris; published reviews in the *Daily Express*; his mother died.

1904   Wrote 'A Portrait of the Artist' on 7 January; published stories in the *Irish Homestead*; taught at the Clifton School, Dalkey; sang in the Feis Ceoil; lived in the Martello Tower, Sandycove; wrote 'The Holy Office'; began *Stephen Hero*; met Nora Barnacle on 10 June; in October they went to Pola in Yugoslavia where he taught English at the Berlitz School.

1905   Taught at Berlitz School in Trieste, Italy; son Giorgio born; brother Stanislaus joined him in Trieste.

1906   Worked as a foreign correspondent at a bank in Rome.

1907   Volume of poems *Chamber Music* published in London; wrote articles in Italian for a Trieste newspaper; daughter Lucia born.

1909   Visited Ireland; established the Volta cinema in Mary St., Dublin, which failed the next year; signed contract with Maunsel & Co. for publication of his volume of short stories *Dubliners*.

1912   Visited Ireland with family; *Dubliners* burnt; wrote 'Gas from a Burner'.

1914   *Dubliners* published in London; *A Portrait of the Artist as a Young Man* serialised in the *Egoist* (London); began *Ulysses*.

1915   Moved to neutral Switzerland; given grant by British Royal Literary Fund.

1916   *A Portrait* published in New York.

1917   First eye operation.

1918   His play *Exiles* published in London; *Ulysses* serialised in the *Little Review* (New York).

1919   *Ulysses* serialised in the *Egoist*.

1920   Moved to Paris; the *Little Review* enjoined from publishing *Ulysses*.

1922   *Ulysses* published by Shakespeare and Company in Paris on 2 February.

1924   Published the first fragment of 'Work in Progress' *(Finnegans Wake)* in the *transatlantic review* (Paris).

1926   *Ulysses* pirated in *Two Worlds Monthly* (New York).

1927   Protest at pirating of *Ulysses* signed by 167 prominent literary personalities; *Pomes Penyeach* published.

1931   Joyce and Nora married in London on 4 July.

1933   New York judge ruled *Ulysses* not pornographic.

1934   Random House edition of *Ulysses* in New York.

1939   *Finnegans Wake* published.

1941   Joyce died on 13 January in Zurich where he was buried.

JAMES JOYCE AND THE NATIONAL LIBRARY

James Joyce can be proudly numbered among the former readers of the National Library of Ireland, which in his day was one of the focal points of literary life in Dublin. Inevitably the National Library must have contributed to his development and some significant proportion of that phenomenal range of learning which his books reveal must surely have been gained via the shelves of the National Library. Joyce may not have been conscious of a debt but he has, nonetheless, immortalised the National Library and some members of its staff in *A Portrait* and in *Ulysses*.

In this the centenary year of the birth of James Joyce it is fitting that the National Library pay some tribute. This collection of facsimiles and photographs is primarily intended for those of any age who have not yet discovered Joyce. For them it may provoke a curiosity and whet an appetite. Long-standing lovers of Joyce may also find it of interest in that it outlines the chronological context of his writings and the principal phases of his life.

The National Library has copies of practically all Joyce's published works, a few of his manuscripts, and a great variety of sources both written and pictorial for the Dublin and Ireland of his time, one of the most important being the well known Lawrence Photographic Collection which records in great detail the Dublin in which he spent his boyhood and youth. All these sources are drawn on for this collection of facsimiles. However, to compile a representative selection of Joyce documents it has been necessary to avail of the resources of a number of other repositories which have kindly cooperated.

We are grateful to the following institutions and individuals for permission to reproduce items in their collections or for advice and assistance in various ways: The Society of Authors, Cornell University Library, Southern Illinois University Library (Carbondale), University of Buffalo Library, University College Dublin Library, Yale University Library, James Joyce Tower Museum, The Irish Independent, The Irish Times, Memo Ltd.; Sheila Asprey, Jimmy Cuthbert, Donald Eddy, John Farrell, Robert Nicholson, Nora O'Shea, Esther Semple, Roma Woodnutt, Marjorie G. Wynne; and to my colleagues in the National Library, especially Teresa Biggins for typing the text, Eugene Hogan for photography, and Brian McKenna for advice on various points of detail in respect of Joyce's life and works.

Noel Kissane,
Education Officer,
National Library of Ireland.

The National Library on the left (beside Leinster House) as it was in Joyce's time. *(Lawrence Collection I. 4208)*